Writing the
U.S. Constitution

by Lori Mortensen
illustrated by Siri Weber Feeney

Picture Window Books
Minneapolis, Minnesota

Special thanks to our advisers for their expertise:
Susanna Robbins, M.A.
Former Assistant Editor, OAH Magazine of History
Terry Flaherty, Ph.D., Professor of English
Minnesota State University, Mankato

Editor: Jill Kalz
Designer: Abbey Fitzgerald
Page Production: Melissa Kes
Art Director: Nathan Gassman
Editorial Director: Nick Healy
Creative Director: Joe Ewest
The illustrations in this book were created with acrylic paint and colored pencil.

Photo Credits: cover (leather texture), Shutterstock/Leigh Prather; 2 (parchment texture), Shutterstock/AGA

Picture Window Books
151 Good Counsel Drive
P.O. Box 669
Mankato, MN 56002-0669
877-845-8392
www.picturewindowbooks.com

Printed in the United States of America.

 All books published by Picture Window Books
are manufactured with paper containing at least
10 percent post-consumer waste.

Library of Congress Cataloging-in-Publication Data
Mortensen, Lori, 1955-
Writing the U.S. Constitution / by Lori Mortensen ; illustrated by Siri Weber Feeney.
p. cm. — (Our American story)
Includes index.
ISBN 978-1-4048-5540-3 (library binding)   7218
1. United States. Constitution—Juvenile literature. 2. United States—Politics and
government—1783-1789—Juvenile literature. 3. Constitutional history—United States—
Juvenile literature. I. Feeney, Siri Weber, ill. II. Title.
E303.M89 2010
342.7302—dc22   2009006895

The United States had won the Revolutionary War, and now it needed its own set of rules. Writing these rules was not going to be easy. In fact, it was going to be one of the new country's most difficult tasks.

UNITE OR DIE

The United States was a new country in 1783. But there was no strong government leading the 13 states. Leaders in each state did things their own way. Some people said the United States was like a monster with 13 heads!

It was time to form a better government. In 1787, a group of men held a special meeting in Philadelphia. It was called the Constitutional Convention.

Leaders from each state were invited. But some states sent no one. Some people did not want to make changes.

Still, many leaders did come. These men were later called the Founding Fathers. George Washington was in charge. James Madison took notes.

Everyone agreed the meeting would be private.
They didn't want to argue in public. So they
closed the windows. They locked the doors.
They posted guards.

The men argued a lot. Everyone had different ideas.

Finally, leaders from Virginia presented the "Virginia Plan." James Madison wrote it.

In the plan, one government would manage all the states. That government would have three parts. One part would lead. Another part would make laws. And another part would make sure the laws were fair. Each state would have votes based on its population.

Some men were shocked by the plan. The government would be too big, they said. States would lose too much power.

Also, leaders from states with small populations were upset. They said it was not fair. They thought small states should have just as many votes as large states!

The men from New Jersey had a plan, too. In it, the U.S. government would have three parts, like the Virginia Plan. But each state would get one vote. Votes would not be based on population.

The plan upset leaders from states with large populations. They said it was not fair. Large states should get more votes!

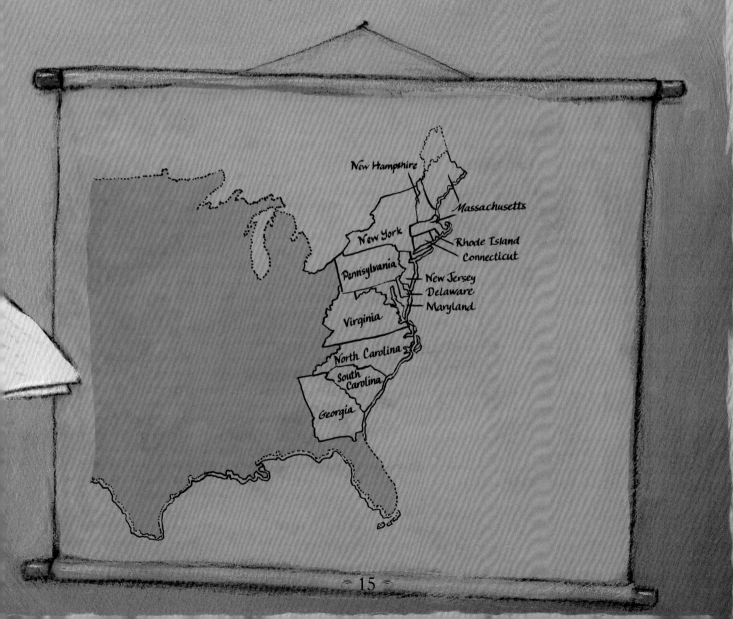

The men argued all summer in the hot room.
They couldn't agree. Some men went home.
It seemed hopeless.

At last the leaders had an idea. They would use parts of both plans. The government would have three parts. But one part would include the Senate and the House of Representatives.

States would have an equal number of members in the Senate. Larger states would have more representatives in the House.

The Three Branches of Government

House of Representatives
Senate
Vice President
Congress
President
Supreme Court
Legislative Branch
Executive Branch
Judicial Branch

The men started putting the ideas on paper.
Each word had to be just right.

They wrote, "We the People …"
These were the first words of the
U.S. Constitution.

The words showed that the
U.S. Constitution was for everyone.
The Constitution included seven
articles, too. The articles explained
how the government worked.

The leaders reviewed what they had written. Some said it still was not good enough. It needed a Bill of Rights, too. This would clearly explain the freedoms of the people. What good was a strong government if it did not protect each person's rights?

But most leaders were ready to go home. The Bill of Rights would have to wait.

On September 17, 1787, the U.S. Constitution was finished. Thirty-nine leaders signed it. At the last minute, three others changed their minds. They would not sign without a Bill of Rights. But it didn't matter. Now the states would decide. If nine states approved it, the United States would have a strong new government.

We the People

The states held their own meetings. They argued and voted. Months went by. The first state to approve was Delaware. Other states followed.

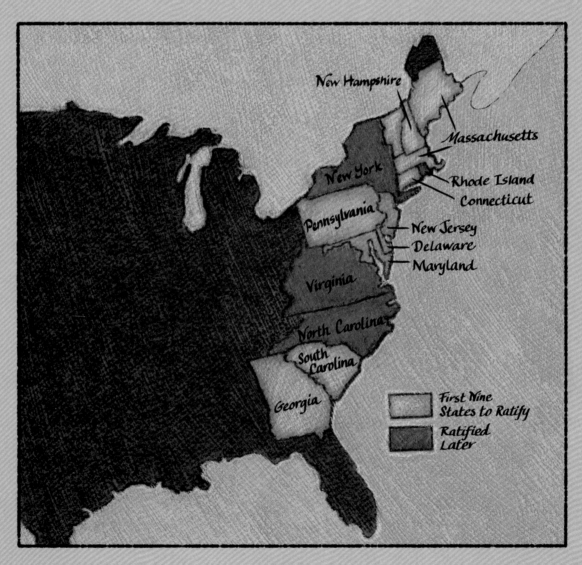

On June 21, 1788, New Hampshire agreed. It was the ninth state. The United States had a new government!

After some time, all the states approved the Constitution. In 1791, the Bill of Rights was added.

The U.S. Constitution was not easy to write. But its powerful words made the United States the strong country it is today.

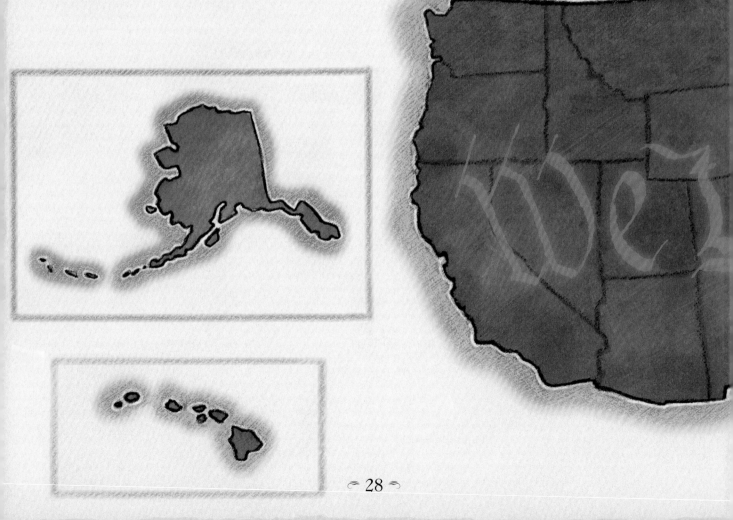

Timeline

1783	The Revolutionary War ends.
1787	The Constitutional Convention takes place in Philadelphia, Pennsylvania. Thirty-nine Convention members sign the U.S. Constitution.
1788	Nine states ratify the U.S. Constitution.
1790	Rhode Island is the last state to ratify.
1791	The Bill of Rights is added.

Glossary

articles—parts of the U.S. Constitution that explain how the government of the United States works

Bill of Rights—the part of the U.S. Constitution that lists the freedoms all U.S. citizens have

House of Representatives—one of the two groups that make up the legislative branch, the part of the U.S. government that makes laws

population—the number of people who live in a place

private—secret

ratify—to approve

Revolutionary War—(1775–1783) the American colonies' fight against Great Britain for freedom

Senate—one of the two groups that make up the legislative branch, the part of the U.S. government that makes laws

U.S Constitution—the plan for how the U.S. government works

To Learn More

⌒ **More Books to Read** ⌒

Catrow, David. *We the Kids: The Preamble to the Constitution of the United States.* New York: Dial Books for Young Readers, 2002.

Cheney, Lynne. *We the People: The Story of Our Constitution.* New York: Simon & Schuster Books for Young Readers, 2008.

Harris, Nancy. *What's the U.S. Constitution?* Chicago: Heinemann, 2008.

Pearl, Norman. *The U.S. Constitution.* Minneapolis: Picture Window Books, 2007.

⌒ **Internet Sites** ⌒

FactHound offers a safe, fun way to find Internet sites related to this book. All of the sites on FactHound have been researched by our staff.

Here's all you do:

Visit *www.facthound.com*

FactHound will fetch the best sites for you!

Look for all of the books in the Our American Story series:

The First American Flag

Paul Revere's Ride

President George Washington

Writing the U.S. Constitution